Peyton Manning

by **Michael Sandler**

Consultant: James Alder
Football Expert
football.about.com

BEARPORT PUBLISHING

New York, New York

Credits

Cover and Title Page, © Doug Murray/Icon SMI/Newscom; 4, © Mike Fender/The Star; 5, © AP Photo/Darron Cummings; 6, © Mark Cowan/UPI/Landov; 7 © Brent Smith/Reuters/ Landov; 8, © Perspective Photos/Steve Geiselman 9, © Perspective Photos/Steve Geiselman; 10, © Bill Frakes/Sports Illustrated/Getty Images; 11, © Bill Frakes /Sports Illustrated/Getty Images; 12, © Ted Jackson/The Times-Picayune/Landov; 13, © John Biever/Sports Illustrated/ Getty Images; 15T, © AP Photo/Michael Conroy; 15B, © SwanLuxury.com; 16, © Boys & Girls Clubs of Rutherford County; 17, © AP Photo/Wade Payne; 18, © James Fasinger/ ABACAUSA.COM/Newscom; 19, © Allen Fredrickson/Reuters/Landov; 20, © AP Photo/Darron Cummings; 21, © Mike Blake/Reuters/Landov; 22L, © KRT/Newscom; 22R, © AP Photo/ Thomas E. Witte.

Publisher: Kenn Goin
Senior Editor: Lisa Wiseman
Creative Director: Spencer Brinker
Photo Researcher: Mary Fran Loftus
Design: Dawn Beard Creative

Library of Congress Cataloging-in-Publication Data

Sandler, Michael, 1965-
  Peyton Manning / by Michael Sandler.
      p. cm. — (Football heroes making a difference)
  Includes bibliographical references and index.
  ISBN-13: 978-1-61772-311-7 (library binding)
  ISBN-10: 1-61772-311-8 (library binding)
  1. Manning, Peyton—Juvenile literature. 2. Football players—United States—Biography—Juvenile literature. 3. Quarterbacks (Football)—United States—Biography—Juvenile literature. I. Title.
  GV939.M289S25 2012
  796.332092—dc22
  [B]

                            2011006636

For more information, write to Bearport Publishing Company, Inc., 45 West 21st Street, Suite 3B, New York, New York 10010. Printed in the United States of America.

070111
042711CGC

10 9 8 7 6 5 4 3 2 1

CONTENTS

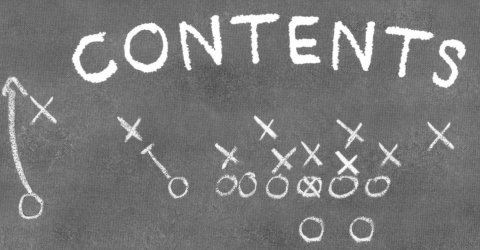

Final Minutes

On January 2, 2011, at Lucas Oil Stadium, the Indianapolis Colts were battling the Tennessee Titans. It was the final game of the 2010–2011 NFL regular season. The Colts needed a win. With it, they would earn their seventh **AFC South** title in eight years.

With just over a minute left in the game, the two teams were tied, 20–20. Colts fans knew what needed to happen next. They had seen it so many times before—their quarterback Peyton Manning leading a game-winning **drive** with the clock ticking down. From inside the Colts' **own territory**, Peyton got ready to work his magic.

Fans at Lucas Oil Stadium, the Colts' home stadium, cheer on Indianapolis.

Peyton (#18) gets ready to throw the ball during the game against the Tennessee Titans.

Peyton Manning is considered by many to be the NFL's greatest **active** quarterback. He has made 11 Pro Bowls, won one Super Bowl, and earned four Most Valuable Player (MVP) awards.

Home Field Hero

Cool and steady, Peyton brought his team downfield. With 1 minute and 18 seconds left on the clock, he hit **receiver** Blair White with a 20-yard (18-m) pass. On the next play, he handed the ball to Joseph Addai for a 6-yard (5-m) gain.

Now there was just over half a minute to go. Peyton quickly connected with **tight end** Jacob Tamme to put the Colts into **field goal range**. Then kicker Adam Vinatieri came in to finish the job. He sent the ball through the **uprights** as time ran out. Score! Thanks to another unbelievable Peyton drive, the Colts had a 23–20 victory and were headed to the playoffs.

Jacob Tamme (#84) heads downfield.

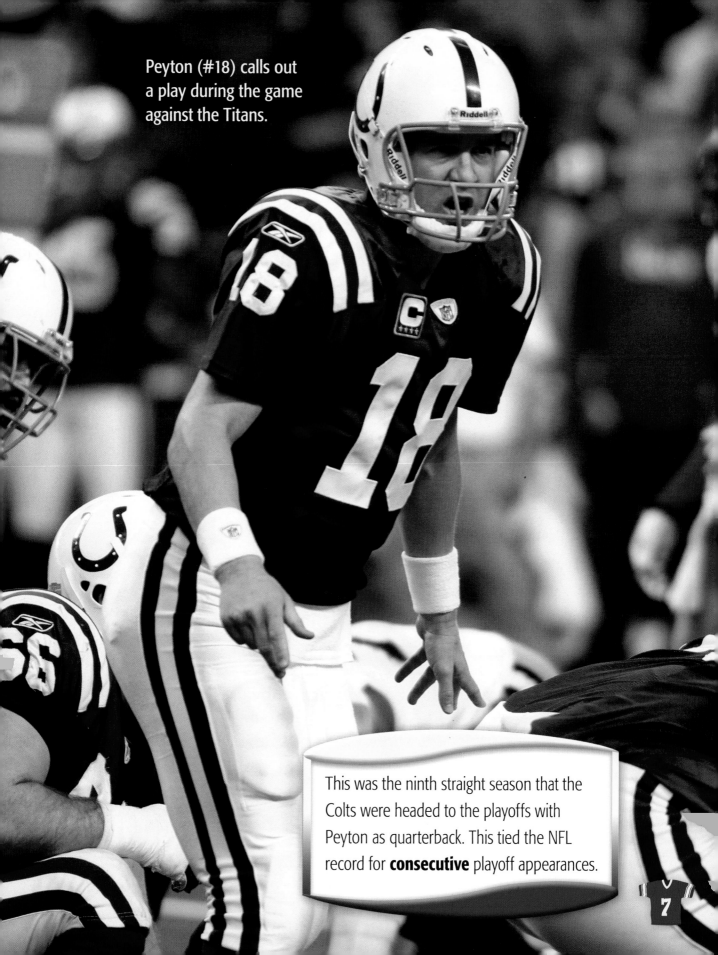

Peyton (#18) calls out a play during the game against the Titans.

This was the ninth straight season that the Colts were headed to the playoffs with Peyton as quarterback. This tied the NFL record for **consecutive** playoff appearances.

A Different Kind of Game

A few months earlier, Peyton had stood on the same football field waiting for another game to begin. Though Peyton wasn't playing in the game, he was just as excited as if he were the **starting** quarterback.

The game that was about to start was part of the PeyBack Classic—an event organized by Peyton that consists of two football games between four Indianapolis high schools. Teenagers, not NFL players, are the stars. For one night, they get the thrill of meeting Peyton and playing on a real NFL field—the scene of so many of Peyton's late-game drives. Peyton has hosted these games since 2000. It's his way of giving back to the local kids who support him.

Peyton talks with some of the players during the PeyBack Classic in 2010.

Two high school teams playing in the 2010 PeyBack Classic

Money raised from ticket sales of the PeyBack Classic goes to help Indianapolis schools and **at-risk** children. The August 20, 2010, PeyBack Classic marked the 11th time Peyton had held the tournament.

Inspiration

Peyton knows how special it is for young players to meet real NFL pros. He had met many himself while growing up in New Orleans, Louisiana.

Peyton's father, Archie Manning, had been an NFL quarterback—a New Orleans Saints passer with a knack for scrambling away from **defenders**. Peyton and his brothers, Cooper and Eli, got to meet many of his father's teammates. Often, after Saints games, Peyton and his brothers would hang out on the field, throwing a ball around. They would pretend to be NFL stars.

For the three brothers, having an NFL pro to learn from was incredibly valuable. When "we asked, he would tell us everything he knew," Peyton said of his father.

The Manning children— (from left to right) Cooper, Peyton, and Eli—stand next to their parents, Olivia and Archie.

Peyton playing for Isidore Newman High School

The experience of meeting and watching NFL pros inspired Peyton as he grew into a star quarterback at Isidore Newman High School in New Orleans.

Camp Manning

Peyton's experiences learning from NFL players continued to help him as he moved on to the University of Tennessee after high school. There, he became one of college football's most **dominant** passers. It was during this time that he got the idea to hold a football camp, where other kids could benefit from the same experiences he had enjoyed growing up.

Soon after, Peyton told his dad about the football camp. Archie thought it was a great idea. In 1996, the Manning Passing Academy was born. Each year since, kids from 8th to 12th grade come from all over the country to attend the four-day-long **clinic** in Louisiana. They have the opportunity to learn offensive skills from Archie, Peyton, Eli, Cooper, and top coaches, many from the NFL. The Mannings even stay in the **dorms** right alongside the campers.

Peyton works with some young quarterbacks at the Manning Passing Academy in 2010.

Peyton in action at the University of Tennessee

Peyton finished his college career as the all-time leading passer for the University of Tennessee's football team.

Paying Back

In 1998, after graduating from college, Peyton was **drafted** by the Colts. Peyton still wanted to do more to give back, so he started the PeyBack **Foundation**. The group's goal is to help **disadvantaged** kids by providing leadership and athletic programs in three locations that are important to Peyton: Louisiana, his home state; Tennessee, where he had played college football; and Indiana, where he lives now.

The PeyBack Classic is just one of the foundation's many activities held in Indianapolis. Another is called Peyton's Pals. With Peyton's help, a group of **foster children** take part in a special activity each month. The kids go on trips to watch basketball or baseball games, and tour colleges. They also participate in **community service** activities such as volunteering at the **Special Olympics**.

The PeyBack Foundation also helps hospitals in Indianapolis. In fact, Peyton helped St. Vincent Children's Hospital so often—by making visits and raising and donating money—that in 2007 the hospital was renamed "Peyton Manning Children's Hospital at St. Vincent."

Peyton greets patients at the Peyton Manning Children's Hospital at St. Vincent.

Peyton poses with patients at the Peyton Manning Children's Hospital at St. Vincent.

Thanks, Tennessee

Both Peyton and his foundation are very active in Tennessee, too. It's where Peyton sharpened his passing skills in college before moving on to the NFL. Twice he has pledged $1 million to the University of Tennessee's athletic department. The money was given to help improve the stadium and training facilities where Peyton had once played football.

Also in Tennessee, the PeyBack Foundation gave **grants** to 25 different groups in 2010. Some of the grants went to schools, aquariums, and zoos. Others went to help pay for sports programs, where kids learn football skills and teamwork. Still others went to groups such as the Boys & Girls Clubs of America, which runs arts, education, and athletic programs to teach skills and responsibility to kids.

Young athletes from the Boys & Girls Clubs of Rutherford County in Tennessee get ready to participate in a day of running events.

Peyton announces his pledge of $1 million to the University of Tennessee on September 5, 2009.

In 2010, the University of Tennessee named a classroom after Peyton Manning because of his strong support for the school.

Louisiana Lifesaver

Of course, there's no place closer to Peyton's heart than his home state of Louisiana. That's where he grew up and learned to play football. In 2010, the PeyBack Foundation gave money to 20 different organizations in Louisiana, mostly in New Orleans. These grants supported groups such as the Second Harvest Food Bank, whose goal is to lead the fight against hunger in southern Louisiana.

Peyton also helped out after Hurricane Katrina struck the state in August 2005. Right after the storm hit, he and his brother Eli rented an airplane. They loaded it with 30,000 pounds (13,608 kg) of medical supplies, baby formula, groceries, and other daily necessities. Then with Peyton, Eli, and other volunteers on board, the supplies were flown from Indianapolis to Louisiana. The supplies would be used to help out the people whose lives had been devastated by the hurricane.

Student volunteers sort food at the Second Harvest Food Bank.

Peyton (left) and Eli (center) talk with a Hurricane Katrina survivor. After Katrina, Peyton said, "I wanted to do whatever I could to help."

In 2010, a huge oil spill polluted the Gulf of Mexico. Many fishermen were put out of work and found it hard to feed their families. Second Harvest helped by giving out more than half a million meals. This type of assistance is the reason that Peyton supports Second Harvest.

Giving Back

Since coming to Indianapolis in 1998, Peyton has earned a Super Bowl champion's ring and more MVP awards than any other player in NFL history. His achievements came about through his pure dedication to the game. While no one works harder than he does, Peyton realizes that others have played a big role in helping him. He credits the love and support he's received from his family and his fans for his success.

This is the reason why Peyton works so hard to help others, and why he tries to bring opportunities to young people in Indiana, Louisiana, and Tennessee. "I was blessed growing up," he says. "Now I want to give back to those kids who have been such terrific fans."

Peyton signs autographs for his young fans.

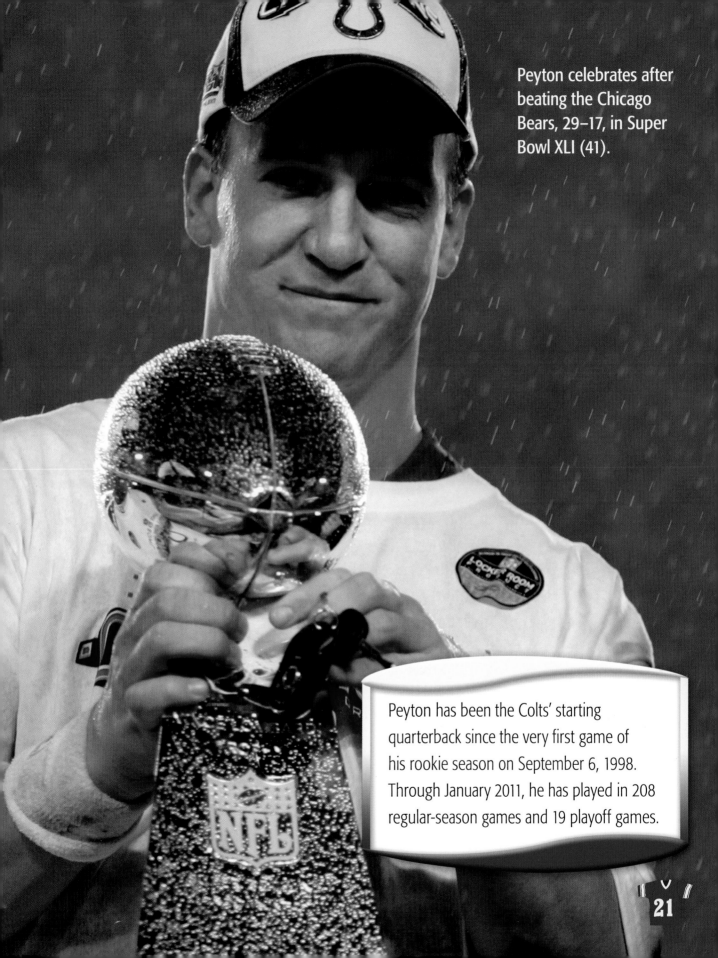

Peyton celebrates after beating the Chicago Bears, 29–17, in Super Bowl XLI (41).

Peyton has been the Colts' starting quarterback since the very first game of his rookie season on September 6, 1998. Through January 2011, he has played in 208 regular-season games and 19 playoff games.

The Peyton File

Peyton is a football hero on and off the field. Here are some highlights.

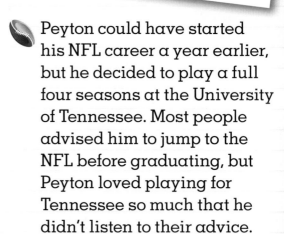

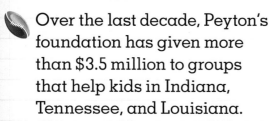 Over the last decade, Peyton's foundation has given more than $3.5 million to groups that help kids in Indiana, Tennessee, and Louisiana.

During the 2010–2011 season, Peyton threw for a career best in passing—4,700 yards (4,298 m). He also set a new NFL record for most **completions** in a season—450.

On January 30, 2011, Peyton played in his 11th Pro Bowl. Brett Favre is the only other quarterback in NFL history to be chosen so many times.

Peyton could have started his NFL career a year earlier, but he decided to play a full four seasons at the University of Tennessee. Most people advised him to jump to the NFL before graduating, but Peyton loved playing for Tennessee so much that he didn't listen to their advice.

Glossary

active (AK-tiv) not retired

AFC South (AY-EFF-SEE SOUTH) one of four divisions in the NFL's American Football Conference (AFC)

at-risk (at-RISK) in danger of having learning, emotional, physical, or behavioral disabilities

clinic (KLIN-ik) a place where kids can go to practice their football skills

community service (kuh-MYOO-nuh-tee SUR-viss) volunteer work done for a good cause

completions (*kom*-PLEE-shunz) passes thrown by the quarterback that are caught by receivers

consecutive (kuhn-SEK-yuh-tiv) in a row

defenders (di-FEN-durz) players who have the job of trying to stop the other team from scoring

disadvantaged (diss-uhd-VAN-tijd) poor and lacking many opportunities

dominant (DOM-uh-nuhnt) one of the very best; capable of controlling a game all by one's self

dorms (DORMZ) rooms where people sleep and live on a college campus

drafted (DRAFT-id) chosen or picked to play for a team

drive (DRIVE) a series of plays in which the team with the ball tries to move down the field

field goal range (FEELD GOHL RAYNJ) an area of the field where a kicker is close enough to be able to make a field goal

foster children (FAWSS-tur CHIL-druhn) children who have to live with other families because their parents are not able to take care of them due to illness or other difficulties

foundation (foun-DAY-shuhn) a group that supports or gives money to worthwhile causes

grants (GRANTS) sums of money given by one group to another group

own territory (OHN TER-uh-*tor*-ee) one team's side of the field; from here, a team has to move the ball to the end of the opposite side of the field to score

receiver (ri-SEE-vur) a player whose job it is to catch passes

Special Olympics (SPESH-uhl oh-LIM-piks) a group that organizes athletic events for children and adults who have intellectual disabilities

starting (START-ing) playing at the start of a game; the best player at a position

tight end (TITE END) an offensive player who catches passes and blocks for other players

uprights (UHP-*rites*) the two upward pointing bars on the goalpost

Bibliography

Corbett, Jim. "Strong Arms and Helping Hands." *USA Today* (February 5, 2010).

Thompson, Ericka P. "Manning PeysBack the Community." *Indianapolis Recorder* (August 22, 2003).

The New York Times

peytonmanning.com

Read More

Sandler, Michael. *Peyton Manning and the Indianapolis Colts: Super Bowl XLI (Super Bowl Superstars).* New York: Bearport (2008).

Sandler, Michael. *Pro Football's Most Spectacular Quarterbacks (Football-O-Rama).* New York: Bearport (2011).

Learn More Online

To learn more about Peyton Manning, visit
www.bearportpublishing.com/FootballHeroes

Index